JOHN THOMPSON'S

FIRST FAVORITES

T0061405

Contents

12286

Teachers and Parents

This collection of First Favorites, written in the John Thompson tradition, is intended as supplementary material for beginning and early elementary level pianists. The pieces may also be used by more advanced students for sight-reading practice. The material is not specifically graded, although pieces appearing later in this book tend to be more demanding than the earlier ones. Dynamics, phrasing and tempo indications have been deliberately omitted, since initially the student's attention should be focused on playing notes and rhythms accurately. Outline fingering has been included, and in general the hand is assumed to remain in a five-finger position until a new fingering indicates a position shift. The fingering should suit most hands, although logical alternatives are always possible.

John Thompson

WILLIS MUSIC

EXCLUSIVELY DISTRIBUTED BY

HAL•LEONARD®
CORPORATION

7777 W. BLUEMOUND RD. P.O. BOX 13819 MILWAUKEE, WI 53213

Illustrations by xheight Limited

House Of The Rising Sun

Space Walk

Michael, Row The Boat Ashore

The Train Is A-Comin' In

Boogie Bug

Red River Valley

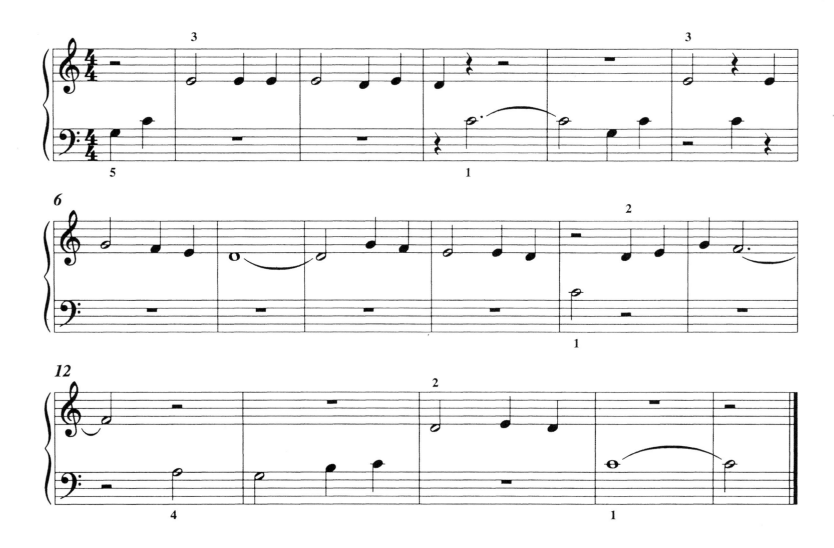

Funky Feline

Go Down Moses

Cool Blue

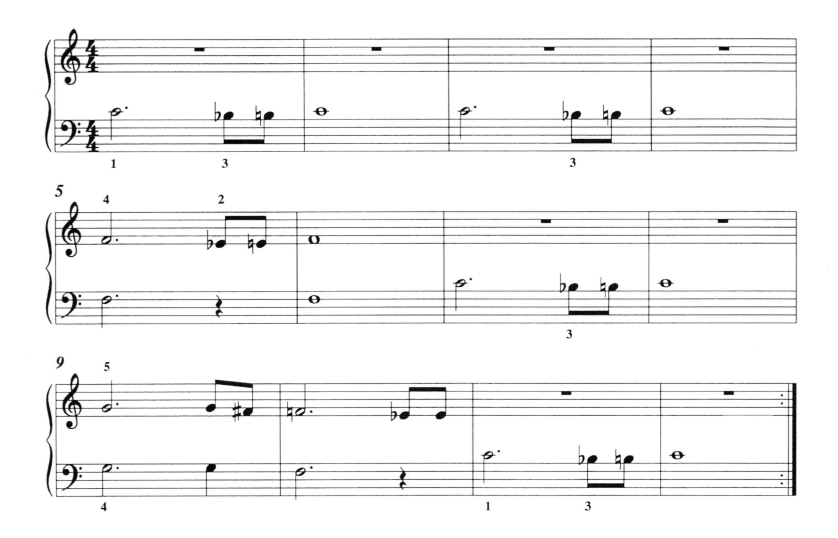

If You're Happy

Nobody Knows The Trouble I've Seen

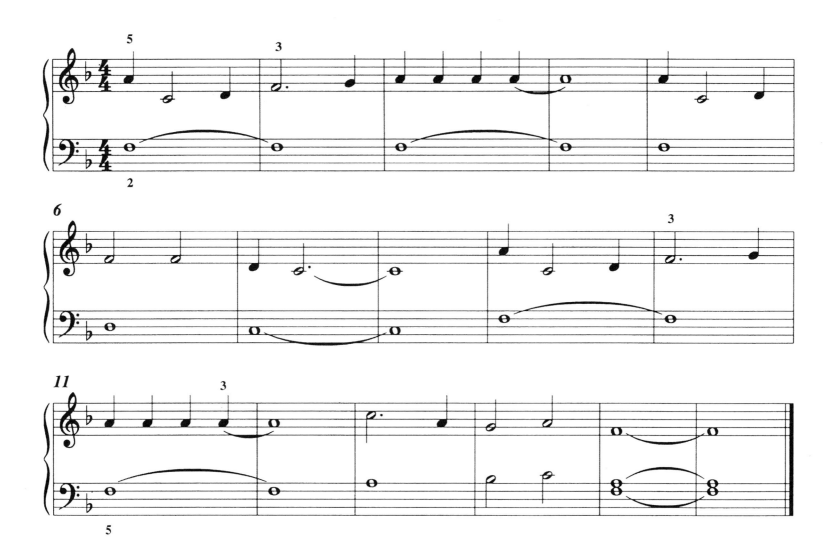

Swing Low, Sweet Chariot

Glad Rag

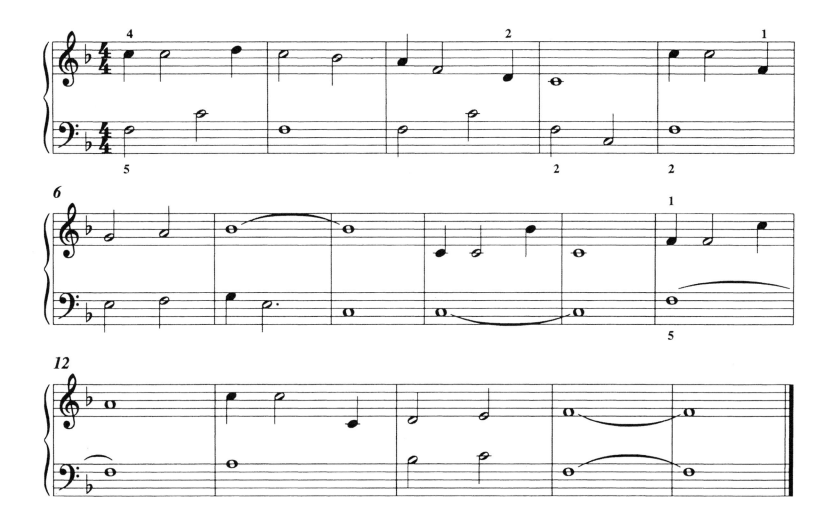

When Johnny Comes Marching Home

Frankie And Johnny

Feelin' Flat Blues

Dixie

Dan Emmett

American Patrol

F. W. Meacham

Night Train

One More River

Banana Boat Song

Walkin' Blues

Oh, When The Saints

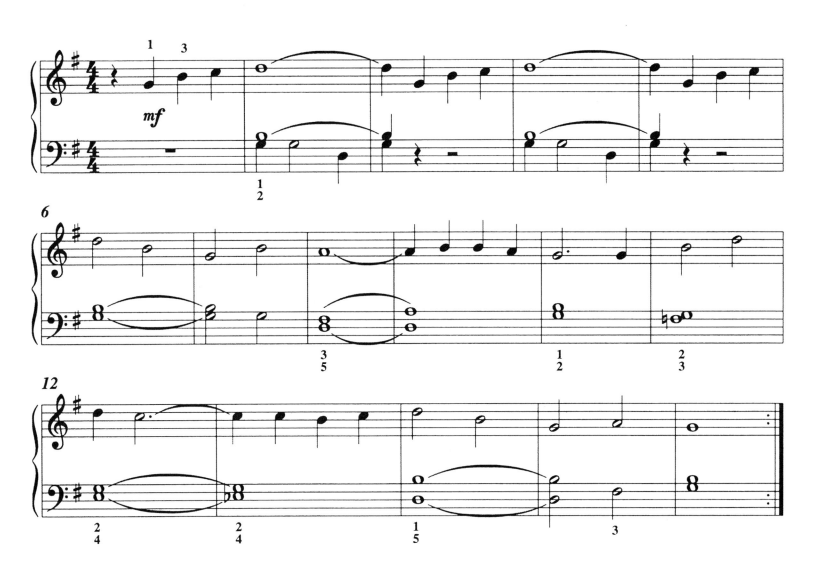

After Dark

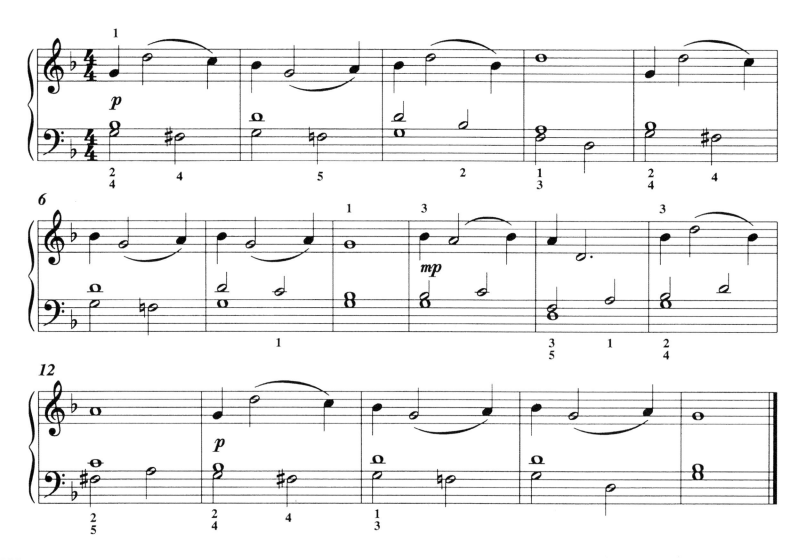

Down By The Riverside

12286

Mexican Hat Dance

Cowboy Blues